Ballad

of the

Beantowne Bosox

*Merry Christmas
Mike
A true blue Red Sox Fan —
Love —
Dad & Mom
Dec. 25th, 2006*

Ballad
of the
Beantowne Bosox

Daniel W. Bates

iUniverse, Inc.
New York Lincoln Shanghai

Ballad of the Beantowne Bosox

Copyright © 2006 by Daniel W. Bates

All rights reserved. No part of this book may be used or reproduced by any means, graphic, electronic, or mechanical, including photocopying, recording, taping or by any information storage retrieval system without the written permission of the publisher except in the case of brief quotations embodied in critical articles and reviews.

iUniverse books may be ordered through booksellers or by contacting:

iUniverse
2021 Pine Lake Road, Suite 100
Lincoln, NE 68512
www.iuniverse.com
1-800-Authors (1-800-288-4677)

ISBN-13: 978-0-595-39456-2 (pbk)
ISBN-13: 978-0-595-83854-7 (cloth)
ISBN-13: 978-0-595-83853-0 (ebk)
ISBN-10: 0-595-39456-6 (pbk)
ISBN-10: 0-595-83854-5 (cloth)
ISBN-10: 0-595-83853-7 (ebk)

Printed in the United States of America

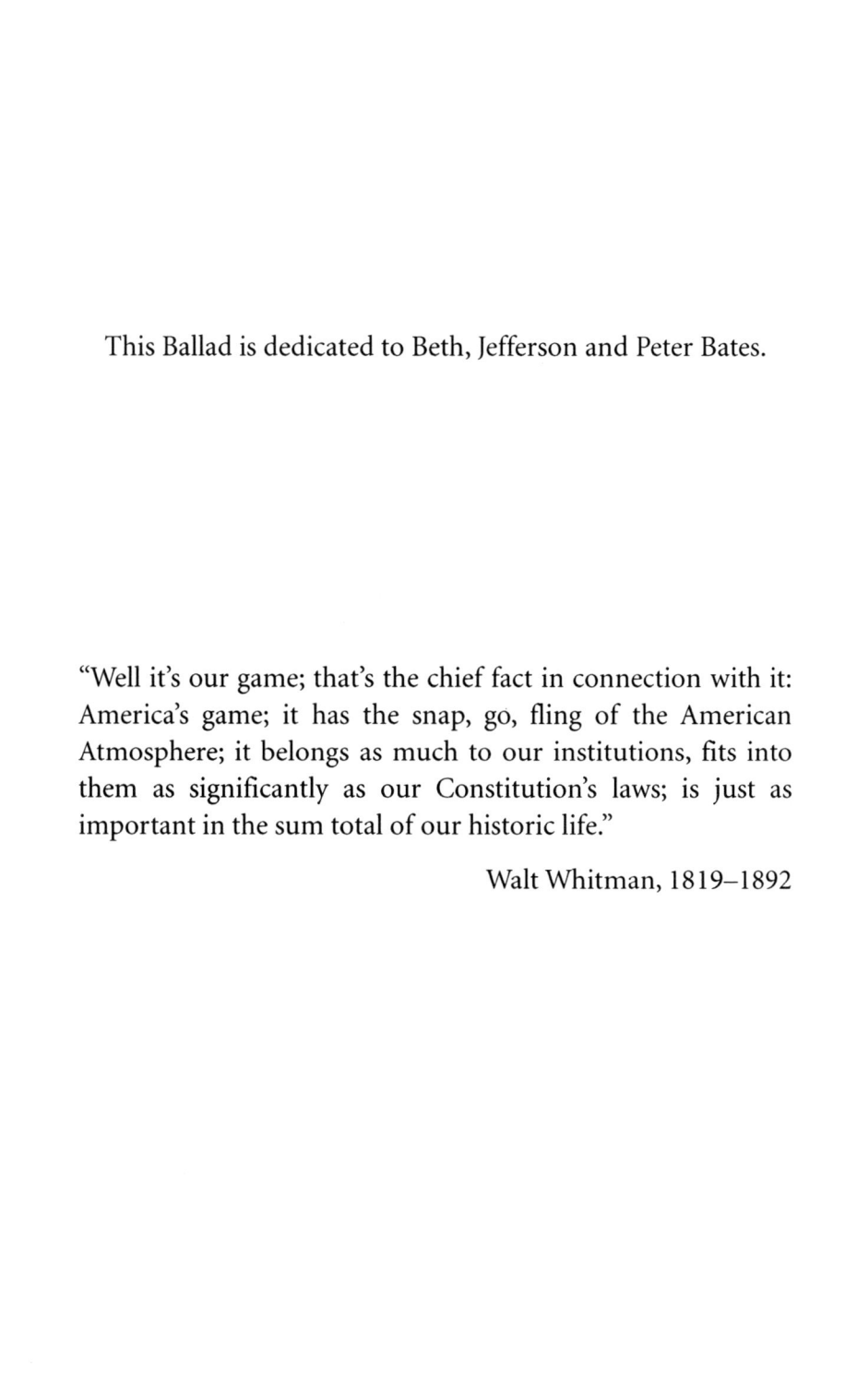

This Ballad is dedicated to Beth, Jefferson and Peter Bates.

"Well it's our game; that's the chief fact in connection with it: America's game; it has the snap, go, fling of the American Atmosphere; it belongs as much to our institutions, fits into them as significantly as our Constitution's laws; is just as important in the sum total of our historic life."

Walt Whitman, 1819–1892

Table of Contents

1. Prelude to Greatness 1
2. Spring, and the Call to Adventure 7
3. Summertime Recreation 13
4. The Magical Autumn of Eleven Heroic Tasks 17
5. Into the Abyss 27
6. Passage out of Night's Realm 31
7. The Fifth Heroic Task 41
8. The Sixth Heroic Task 51
9. The Seventh Heroic Task 65
10. The One-Hundredth World Series 75
11. The Ninth Heroic Task 81
12. The Tenth Heroic Task 87
13. The Eleventh and Final Heroic Task 93
14. Return to the Homeland's Jubilant Parade 101
About the Ballad 107
About the Author 109

Acknowledgements

The author gives thanks to Beth Bates for her love, spirit, enthusiasm and brilliance; to the poets Scott Bates, Sir Walter Scott, E.A. Robinson, H.W. Longfellow, Ogden Nash, Robert Frost, Ghandi and James Taylor; to the Gentlemanly Icon Jim Lonborg for snapping his World Series Ring; to historic and poetic consultants Danny Smith, John Fitzsimmons and Judy Maldovan; to Red Sox Fans, Experts and Consultants Albion Ricker, Bill Trask, Robert Porteous III, John Lemieux and George Heselton. Thanks to Mom the Writer and Dad, the Wordsmith who took me to my first game with Tommy and Lar.

The author also wishes to especially thank Gary Crocker, a genuine Maine Character with a lifelong love for the Red Sox since his first visit to Fenway in '58 as a Little Leaguer from North Monmouth, Maine. After growing up some, he was part of the Navy crew that lifted Celtics parquet for Bruins ice at the Garden. Gary recently performed the Ballad on CD in the voice of the Downeast Character for which he's deservedly famous and loved. The CD is now available by calling, toll-free, 1-87-SOX-POEM-1 or checking out www.BeantowneBallad.com

For the immortal words of Tom Hanks: "There's no crying in baseball!," the author wishes to thank Columbia Pictures' "A LEAGUE OF THEIR OWN", © 1992 Columbia Pictures Industries, Inc. All Rights Reserved. Courtesy of Columbia Pictures.

1. PRELUDE TO GREATNESS

Listen my children, and you shall hear
Of a Team and a Towne and a Heck of a Year.
'Twas the 16th of April, Two Thousand Four
When the BoSox of Beantowne kicked off some Lore.

The Red Sox are looking to Win It All
And have gathered the Guys to do it;
Guys with Spirit and Mighty Strength
The gods of Myth even knew it.

These mischievous gods of Baseball Fate
Sitting 'round spinning the breeze,
Are talking 'bout Millar's Spirit
And the Power of David Ortiz,

Talkin' 'bout Bellhorn's boyhood dreams
'Bout Nixon's and Schilling's health,
Discussing Manny's Mighty Bat
And Damon's hustle and stealth.

Of Pedro's tidy E.R.A.,
How Mueller fields the Fens;
Of pitching talent colossal enough
To fill about five bull-pens.

Combined, their Spirited, Noble Hearts
Create a Transcendent Power!
Plus these Guys have a Handshake Thing
That takes a half an hour!

"What'd be wacky," said one of these gods,
"Would be if the Commish'd proclaim
The Series advantage goes to the League
Whose team wins the All-Star Game!

"And then have Roger Clemens,
The National League Ace thereat,
Pitch his League to a six-run hole
Right off the baseball bat!"

And thus the Code and Affairs of Men
Are Cosmicly Preordained,
The Sun, the Moon and Stars are set
For Team Greatness to be Regained!

2. SPRING, AND THE CALL TO ADVENTURE

The Sox Season is a mountain road
Of Berkshirian Dimension
Whose ups and downs show the Stuff
Of their Ultimate Ascension.

For time and again against the Yanks
As they journey these crests and vales
Eternal Truths of Fellowship
Blaze Team-Wide, Upward Trails.

Over this time, Forged are the Bonds
Of this Commonwealth's Common Good.
"Be the change you wish in the World"
Are words by the Sox understood.

Each came from a faraway place of birth
To Fenway to congregate,
Where Spirited Deeds and Common Will
Converge at a Hallowed Home Plate!

The Plate where stood Teddy Williams,
Where batted the Great Babe Ruth,
The Plate of Yaz and Fisk, Boggs and Rice;
Of Conigliaro's Youth.

The timeless cornerstone of the Fens
O'er which, to win the Cy Young,
Lonborg would sling that evasive sphere
Past guys who'd miss when they swung!

Some say that God made this Game
To test, o'er the course of a year,
The measure of each singular Man,
Against his numerical peer.

Like ribbies or hits with guys on base,
Or slugging percentage, or homers
But to the gods of Baseball Fate
These numbers are numbing misnomers.

Team Play, not numbers, is what achieves.
It's Spiritual in the Fens.
The Towne and the Team, Pulling as One
From the opening camera lens!

On April Sixteenth, the Sox beat the Yanks.
Beat them on prime time T.V.
Over the year beat 'em a bunch of times;
Kicked the butt of this Rivalry!

The Oldest Rivalry Known to Man,
Evil destroyed by Good!
"Isness" converges with "oughtness"
At a point where horsehide meets wood!

Where horsehide meets wood and grass meets cleats,
A grass where Heroes Strode,
And stride as Well To This Very Day,
In this Heavenly Fenway Abode!

In a billion children's dreams is where
You stand in the Box as Ortiz.
You Blast a fastball down and inside
To bring a dragon to its knees.

You win the game with a single,
A homer or throw to First.
For this the Sox are born to live,
For this they greatly thirst!

3. SUMMERTIME RECREATION

All the Sox fight and toil and win;
Downing Dragons with Comraderie!
Yet through the Season's first four months
They must also fight gravity.

Nine games South of the Yanks the Sox are,
When on July 24th;
Down ten to eight late in the game,
The Sox start heading North.

Bronson Arroyo, by mistake
Smacks A-Rod with one of his pitches
Who steps to the mound in such a way
As might leave Arroyo in stitches!

But A-Rod stops, just as his face
Gets a whole lot mittier,
When Varitek's mitt he slugs with his face!
(By contrast the mitt is prettier.)

From that point on, the Sox kick butt,
Win that one eleven to ten.
They win their way to the finish,
Gaining heroes time and again!

From the common abyss that ended '03;
From the dark of this midseason hole;
These Men are gathered from Worlds Away
To Create a Single Soul.

Is this an Earthly or Cosmic Quest
Towards best by every measure?
To Heaven's "is" from Earth's "has been";
Every gathering a treasure?

Straight through they win to the Fenway Finale,
When the Yanks come visiting Boston,
To suffer at the hands of the Sox
An eleven to four accostin'!

Bean counters in Bean Towne compare the Sox ;
Wins against losses regarded
Against the records across the League.
Boston gets Wild Carded!

The Call to Adventure thus answered
The First Pitch of Greatness Tossed!
The Passage out of History's Night;
Its Threshold Celestially Crossed!

4. THE MAGICAL AUTUMN OF ELEVEN HEROIC TASKS:
October 5, 2004

Anaheim, Game 1

Paired against Anaheim in the West,
A team with great hitting power.
Though they play the Angels on Western Turf,
The Sox are the Dudes of the Hour.

Game One commences at Anaheim.
Washburn pitches; the Angelic Ace.
In the Fourth he not only faces Ortiz
But Every Red Sox's Face!

He walks Ortiz; Millar blasts one out!
Three Sox then load up the bases!
Figgins then throws Damon's grounder
To the backstop, of all places!

Two runs sprint home; two Sox are on.
To bat comes The Powerful Manny,
Who can hit it to any nook in the Park,
Who can hit it to any cranny.

The cranny he picks is past Center,
Out of the Park for Three!
When the Fourth Inning's done, it's Eight to One
After the Sox's Lively Spree!

Somewhere in there is the Winning Run!
The Sox take it three to nine!
Schilling Pitched Great, but his Ankle's fate
Is twisted and borderline.

Anaheim, Game 2

Pedro is pitching to start Game Two
Throwing Ninety-Six Miles Per!
The Hitting Momentum that Powers the Sox,
No Angel can ably deter.

Varitek Homers for Two in the Sixth
Into the Right-Field Pavilion.
Thoughtful is he, to thus tie the Game,
Without nailing a civilian.

Then in the Ninth with a Sock on Each Base
And the Sox ahead by two,
Cabrera clobbers a two-base hit!
At Home, three Sox rendezvous!

The Sox are playing Quality Ball:
Ball that doesn't trouble you.
They fly to Boston on the Power and Lift
Supplied by that Second W.

To The Fens: Game Three

They fly to the Fens, the source of their Power
This Temple of Rapturous Dance.
Back to the Crystal Chrysalis,
The Home of their summer advance.

Back to the Fans who search by the Light
Of the Wisdom of their Hearts,
Who rejoice in Fenway's slatted seats,
Rejoice in the sum of its parts;

Who rejoice in its fragrance of popcorn and franks,
Rejoice in its breath and its voice!
In its Field and Wall, so green and tall,
In its Emerald Diamond they Rejoice!

The Fight at the Fens may be characterized
As an old-fashioned donnybrook.
For every blow the Red Sox Dealt,
One of equal measure they took.

Bronson Arroyo is Perfect for three
'Tis the third when the Sox first scored.
Ramirez and Nixon get two R.B.I.s
With Ortiz and Bellhorn aboard.

The Angels score one in the top o' the fourth.
The Red Sox answer with three,
As Mueller and Damon and Bellhorn get on,
The next run is a fait accompli,

'Cause Manny Ramirez Sacrifice Flies.
Mueller gets Duly Plated!
Ortiz lines a shot o'er Guerrero's head,
Second base gets appropriated.

Two runs score; it's five to one
As Bronson keeps mowing 'em down!
The Corn-Row Kid's a Hero for six,
Well deserving that renown.

It's six to one in the seventh.
Arroyo is given a rest.
Then Myers and Timlin load the bags
To bring up the Angels' best.

Guerrero can really blast the ball
Only Boston has said he can't.
'Cause up to that point Red Sox Pitching
Made him look like the Potted Plant.

Not the case this time around,
("Around" is the operative word;)
For around the bases, four Angels jog,
As if a Grand Slam just occurred.

'Cause that's exactly what Guerrero does:
He homers in four R.B.I.s,
The fourth of which renders the Game
The most thrilling of nail-biting ties.

Bitten-off nails pile up in the Fens
Into an Extra Inning.
The six-to-six score for three innings more
Gives no clue as to who'll be winning!

Then in the tenth, with a mate on first
Ortiz does a Thing to the Ball
To send it over the Opposite Field
With Power to Clear the Green Wall!

He Biffs it, Bashes it, Crushes and Crashes it!
Smashes and Smites That Thing!
That Ball is Pasted, Popped and Lambasted
With one Patented, Powerful Swing!

That ball is gone before Ortiz
Takes a step and a half towards first.
That Ball flies to Infinity
On that Tremendous Muscular Burst!

Thousands of Fans at the Crack of his Bat
Follow the Ball's Outflow,
And then with Ortiz and the Whole Happy Team
Celebrate that Hit's Afterglow!

With two runs in and the Game a Win
And the Song of that Sweep a Success,
The Glow of the Sweep sweeps into the Fans'
Blissful Consciousness!

5. INTO THE ABYSS

The first three Yank games are a Bummer.
We've seen it. We've read about it;
The pleasant antidote for which
Is just to fuggedaboutit!

6. PASSAGE OUT OF NIGHT'S REALM

Fast forward; October Seventeenth
The Sox down three games to O
The Yanks get two in Inning Three
On a one-on A-Rod blow.

But Lowe hangs tough, it's inning five
Mueller walks, then so does Millar
Cabrera hits as mellow a hit
As a 2000 Pinot Noir.

That single drives in Mueller.
Manny moves the runners anew.
Ortiz clutches out another hit
To erupt the Fenway Venue!

Orlando tears home from second,
While Millar jogs in from third.
Round every corner of Red Sox World
'Twas a shot that everyone heard!

But the Yanks get one in the top of the sixth
When Williams and Clark get singles.
So four runs to three stands the score
Of a Game that gives the gods tingles.

Down three games to 0, and four runs to three
One might view this with some dread
But one of such mind, thus inclined
Is not wearing Red Sox red!

The Yanks are up four to three in the ninth.
Millar fights for a walk.
Roberts pinches for Kevin to run at first,
Watching Rivera like a hawk.

The matchless skills of Roberts
Can divine with clear insight
The mind's eye of Rivera
Before his feet take flight.

With his eye on Rivera's smallest move,
With insight and exaction;
His gut is trained to know the point
To translate instinct into action.

Roberts gets paid to study this guy;
In gauging his moves he's well-versed.
Roberts looks right into Rivera's brain.
Thrice there's a bullet to first.

Roberts gets back easy, then edges
From first on his toes,
Sizes up pitcher and catcher,
On the pitch to home Roberts goes!

Roberts takes off like an ass-shot duck!
Posada throws hard to Jeter!
In all of Baseball History,
Would a safe sign ever look sweeter?

Touched by the wing-footed Mercury,
The god of speed and hustle,
He digs for the Archetypal Steal
Drawing on every muscle.

To be able to call upon one who can take
The wind and make it his,
At a Time of Matchless Consequence
Is what Team Greatness is!

For a man to sprint with lightning speed
To insure his people's survival,
Is a Primal, Ageless, Timeless Thing
And here meant his Team's revival!

The toss is perfect! The tag by the book!
But a face-slide avoids disaster!
As hard as the throw; as quick the glove's sweep,
Dave is a facial hair faster!

The instant the skin of Roberts' hand
Touches canvas of second base,
The sweep of the leather's a fraction away
From the tag that leg would outrace!

The ump sees that touch from two feet away,
Makes wings with his arms and his hands!
Showing the World Roberts' stuff!
Manifesting it for the fans!

Roberts leads off as Mueller steps in.
He swings and takes off from the plate
Around Rivera that playful ground ball
Commences to navigate!

That ball makes center! Roberts off like a shot
Rounds third through turf and loam,
Chuggin' to home, slides 'cross the plate
To a Team Hug just south of Home.

Those Puckish gods of Baseball Fate,
Lounging in fields of clover,
Were inventing the Curse of the Berra:
"It ain't over 'till it's over!"

Fenway Park is going nuts
The score tied four to four
The Sox bring in seven pitchers.
The Yanks would score no more.

The Pen gives the Sox six innings
Of Os on the Monster Board
Stacking up Yanks like cordwood
'Till the twelfth brings a sweeter chord.

Manny cranks a leadoff single,
Inviting Papi up to bat,
Who never needs instruction
On where the top o' the Wall is at.

Philosophically for Dave Ortiz,
Life's Obvious Highest Reason
Is smacking your hands together hard
And hitting homers all post-season!

Quantrill from the mound throws a ball and a strike
And then throws another ball.
Ortiz, with his Patented Power Cut
Creams the next pitch way AWOL!

What euphoric happiness this?
Hearts soar 'long the Charles and Mystic
Soar to euphoric Baseball Bliss!
All New England goes Ballistic!

All of Red Sox Nation watched
As that ball the outfield cleared
Scattering Yanks—the Fans giving thanks
For the Big Man with the skinny beard!

Ortiz is half-way to first by now
Pointing Skyward; Grinning wide,
The Red Sox dugout empties and views
His exuberant Home-Run Stride!

He touches second and touches third
Preparatory to some High Glovin'!
He jumps on Home, to the South of which
He gets a ton of Red Sox Lovin'!

'Twas October eighteenth, one twenty a.m.
The Yanks looked like they'd been through a shredder
So a few hours' pause was granted before
Game two of that day's Double-Header.

7. THE FIFTH HEROIC TASK:
October 18th and 19th, 2004

Pedro zips through half an inning
Then Mussina takes the mound.
Cabrera singles—the fans go wild!
Manny greatly approves of that sound.

So Manny cracks a single too,
Bringing up Ortiz,
Who's continuing his Clinic
'Bout hittin' in Ribbies with ease!

Now when Sox are down three games to one
And you call upon Ortiz,
History in ages past
Might be thinking Cervantes.

But Myth will never in Ortiz's hands
Tilt at Windmills powered by breeze.
The Figure he will always cut
Will be that of Hercules!

So with Manny Ramirez safely aboard
And Orlando in scoring position,
Mussina kicks and delivers to
The Dominican Ribbie Clinician.

Dave blasts a single, sweet and timely.
Cabrera sprints in to score.
Mussina loads the bases,
With the Red Sox looking for more.

All three bags are chock full o' Sox
For Jason Varitek,
Who fights for a walk, Manny walks home;
A Ribbie! What the heck!

Williams homers in the second
To make it two to one
Then Pedro pitches scoreless ball
With a fastball like a gun.

Add to that those cutting curves
That dance and goof around
Before they reach the strike zone
Sixty big ones from the mound.

And what seems to be most pleasing
To the Folks of Red Sox Nation,
Not only does that baseball cut;
It cuts to great location.

Three Yanks get on in the top of the sixth.
Jeter gets the wussiest double.
Three runs get in. It's four to two,
Waking the guys with the facial stubble.

In particular Papi Ortiz
Who'd homered quite early that day.
He now crushes one over the Monster Seats
That lands a mile from Yawkey Way.

That ball isn't just Fair, it's Excellent,
And brings the Sox to down four to three.
All they need now is a couple of runs
To capture a victory.

Millar then walks. Roberts then subs.
Trott trots him to third with a single.
Varitek cranks a fly, Roberts tears home
To a South-of-Home-Tying-Run Mingle!

The innings go extra. Then came Bronson
Arroyo in the tenth strikes out Jeter!
You'd guess that A-Rod, at twenty-five mil
Could put some wood on the ball neater.

But they overpay A-Rod for that at bat!
The Cornhead strikes him out too!
Then he gets Sheffield to pop out just like
Zippo the clown might do.

Then Wakefield pitches! The Ball Goes Nuts!
With properties not fully known,
It boogies, break-dances, zips north and south
Gettin' jiggy in the strike zone.

That ball does a twirl, a parry, a feint
When Wakefield omits the spin!
To the batter it looks like the Boston Ballet
After slightly too much gin.

Or like Bird fakin' to Ainge but hittin' McHale,
Or the puck on the stick of Bourque,
Or like Brady and Branch fakin' three backs
Into a clockwise torque!

The ball's seam just seems to be grinning
As it advances, all unspinned,
A baffler of baseball's very best bats,
A Plaything of the Wind.

When that ball gets halfway home,
Whatever the batter's pluck
He still is looking for some kind of clue
'Bout whether to swing or duck!

There's nothing as funny as watching a Yank
Doin' a pretzel gyration,
With slapstick heretofore reserved
For Disney animation!

Wakefield delivers three innings
Of knucklers all over the place!
'Twixt playful ball and wailin' bat
Are colossal measures of space.

In the bottom of the fourteenth frame
Damon works a one-out walk.
As does Manny, with the outs at two,
Moving Johnny closer to chalk.

With Damon at second, the <u>very</u> last guy
You'd want to pitch pitch four-sixty-two to,
Would probably be David Ortiz
'Cause of all the stuff your team he could do to!

But unfortunately for the Yanks
Ortiz is next in the order,
A fact held dear by every fan
Outside the New York border.

Poor Loaiza pitches pitch after pitch
Fielders planted against the wall
That's the spot where they figure
Ortiz'll power the ball.

Ortiz toys with the guy for nine pitches
Then with skilled but fun-loving demeanor
He takes a swing and pokes a li'l
Bloopy, loopy 'Tweener!

Floating to a place 'tween outfield and in,
What had been pitch four-seventy-one
Lands out of the reach of nine well-placed Yanks
Who guessed Papi would hit it a ton.

That ball touches grass as Damon rounds third!
He's off like a butt-shot Puma!
He speeds home with the artful grace
Of Thurman, (not Munson but Uma.)

Exuberance reigns all over the Park,
And in every Red Sock Mind!
Again there's Team Lovin' just South of Home
Of a Joyful but Masculine Kind!

Down three to O two nights ago,
The team fights to win five to four.
They're One Enchanted Evening away
From Enchantedly Evening the Score!

8. THE SIXTH HEROIC TASK:
October 19th, 2004

The Sox want Schilling to pitch Game Six.
A guy with Heart and Style
An Ace of a pitcher and a heck of a Guy
Who pitches Location with Guile.

But the way his right tendon is painfully bendin'
The pain it's sendin' is real
There's no pretendin' that its lack of mendin'
Is endin' that painful feel.

The choice remains pendin' with the Team Doc lendin'
Tendon mendin' advice:
"Pull just one suture—Curt's immediate future
Will blend guts with a pitch that flies nice."

With his ankle thus mendin' the Red Sox are sendin'
Curt to the mound in New York.
From that mound he's ascendin' his pitches are tendin'
To pop like a Champagne cork.

Curt stacks up outs like pancakes
(Metaphorically speaking.)
His guts and drive keep the Sox alive
Through the first third of the win they're seeking.

But through three innings the Sox can't get
A runner around four bases.
For once their hitting's as hairy
As are their unshaven faces.

With Kevin Millar at second base,
And outs then totaling two
Varitek steps up to the plate
Batting the Old Switcheroo.

Jason looks at strike one, then strike two.
Lieber throws one by Posada!
Kevin Millar zips over to third
O'er the base path of terracotta.

Varitek works the count for a tad
Taking two balls, fouling off four.
Then cleanly singles to center field
As Millar trots in for the score.

Cabrera singles. Two men are on.
Then Bellhorn, Boston-Born-And-Bred,
Steps to the Plate of History
To bat for the Sox of Red.

He hits one, <u>kablooie,</u> well over Matsui
And into a fan wearing black.
A bona fide homer to sports fans all over
Even fans watching tube in the shack.

The only four folks in the hemisphere;
The only four folks in the park
Who don't give Bellhorn the homer
Are the Umps in clothing of dark.

So the Umps commence to confabulate,
While one pulls his cell from his pocket,
And asks directory assistance
For his cousin in Millinocket.

He knew that Corkie'd be watching the Game:
Hunting's over when the sun sets.
Or at least his wife Mavis would see it,
Assuming that Cable she gets.

"So how's Mavis's tooth?" the Ump begins
Askin' 'bout Corkbeezer's spouse.
As the millions of T.V. viewers watch
Mark's homer leaving The House.

"It's fine" said his Cousin 'bout Mavis's tooth.
"How're things down at where you are?"
"Good" says the Ump "But might I just ask…"
"Wait" says Cork "while I stow my cigar."

"Cork," says the Ump, "we're not allowed
To check out the replay and such,
But if you've got cable and can check out the play
I'd appreciate it very much."

"Course we got cable. You're on my T.V.
And you'd better make a decision.
Every Red Sox and Yank fan Nationwide
Awaits your thoughtful precision."

"I've just got a query" the Umpire asked,
"Whether Bellhorn hit it out."
"Let me ask Mavis," Corkie replied,
"I was making paté out of trout,"

"So I was distracted. YO MAVIS" he yelled
As Yankeedom bit its nails.
"Did Bellhorn's fly ball clear the wall?"
"By two yahds," she responsively wails.

Corkie relays the news to his cousin the Ump,
Saying "Mavis saw the replay slow-mo,"
By which he meant that Mavis's last toddy
May have distorted the show.

No matter, because the satellite line
Using Millinocket cellular power
Relayed "It's a homer, sure as your nose,"
To New York from that cellular tower.

So the Ump who's Corkie's cousin
Signals Bellhorn 'round the bases.
Varitek and Cabrera both touch home
As to Home that Boston Boy paces.

Bellhorn thus chalks up three ribbies!
It's four to zip. Boston's up!
As Schilling again Transcends the Mound
His purpose to Yankee-whup!

Schilling sets up the Yankees with sliders,
Thrilling a blissful Red Sox Nation
Keeping it low, throwing split-finger stuff;
Stuff of Studied Location.

He pitches poetry in the fourth and fifth;
Permits through the sixth not a run.
Instead of an arm and an ankle
It's like Curt's got a laser gun.

When a man thus transcends his mortal self,
Transcends the abyss of game one,
Goes to a faraway land like the Bronx
And pitches a Megaton;

When a man sets out to achieve a good
Defends Home to the last rampart;
When he slays the thing that brought his Land waste
And brings back that Dragon's Heart;

Throwing Lightening, Throwing Swords of Fire,
To Slay the Cosmic Beast;
Each pitch speaking eloquence
Each batter thus Golden Fleeced;

When placing such a man as this
In a Like-Souled Congregation,
The gods thus bring to it's Towne a Team
Of Timeless Veneration.

Thus Schilling and his Teammates
Record six innings of zeros,
On their way to that lofty place
Of Great Mythological Heros.

To describe this Man and the Men he's amongst;
"Legendary" is not a misnomer.
Curt struck out four and allowed just one run
On a measly Williams homer.

So Schilling Retires in Glory
After kicking Yankee poyo
To Kick some more, Francona calls
On Corn-Row-Kid Arroyo.

The Bronson-Dude is Pitchin' Hard
But Jeter makes it to first.
Then A-Rod hits a chopper
Which to the Corn-Row-Kid traversed.

Arroyo grabs it easily,
Sprints over to tag the Yankee,
When A-Rod decides to give the ball
A spineless, sissified spankie!

He swats the ball from Bronson's glove,
Running outside the part that's grassless,
A move Ty Cobb might even regard
As ugly and utterly classless.

Jeter skitters around the bags
As the ball skitters down the line.
Rodriguez skitters to second
With a bogusness infantine.

About a bazillion viewers at home
See A-Rod commit interference;
But inside Yankee Stadium
This view has few adherents.

Except for the fair-minded Red Sox of course,
And their fair-minded, brave supporters,
And the Umps, who meet to spin the breeze
At their first-base-line headquarters.

Into which, to add a spin of his own
Rodriguez inserts his person.
But for every heated word he speaks
His worthiness seems to worsen.

He seeks to persuade the Men in Black
Of the creative but goofy notion,
That his sissified flail at Bronson's glove
Was his natural running motion.

Fans are yellin' from the bleachers!
They're yammerin' from the box!
Imploring the A-Rod to deceive
The Umps to cheat the Sox!

But it must be good to be an Ump
And tell an imposing pest
Even if he makes twenty-five mil;
"Hey Butt-Wad, give it a rest;

"You're going back to the dugout!
"Jeter's going back to first!
"You're out with a ninety-yard penalty!"
The Umps ordered, uncoerced.

The Yankee crowd threw a tantrum
On their pin-striped team's behalf
Like fifty thousand whiney-butts
Of average age three-and-a-half.

Even some gods of playful fate
Who'd been Yankee fans for years,
Raise an eyebrow at this performance
And worse, put down their beers!

'Tis then they realize the Spheres
Of Baseball's Foreordainment
Must make its Loftiest Victory
A Noble and Just Attainment.

For "there's no crying in Baseball!"
In the words of the immortal Hanks,
And a Ball-Park's confines are Friendly
Per the Deity Ernie Banks.

And when these Truths become disturbed
And Baseball's play becomes uneased,
When it's Spheres become misaligned
Baseball's gods become displeased!

'Tis then those just and playful gods
And manager Francona,
Bring in from the Pen to work his stuff
Their Ace Reliever Persona

To end the game. Clark swings and whiffs
With one of his mighty strokes
At the mightily-hurled fast-ball
Of the Great That's All Foulkes.

With Spirited and Noble Hearts
This Team leads Red Sox Nation
To a four-to-one Victory,
And Blissful Jubilation!

As the games thus even three to three,
As to a seventh the Sox fight toward,
They prove their Pen is Mightier
Than the Yanks, who through three had soared.

9. THE SEVENTH HEROIC TASK:
October 20th, 2004

The Yankees win in seven?
The Sox are thinking not.
Not with the J-Man Batting
In the Red Sox lead-off spot.

Up to that point Damon's bat
Reposed, as if in slumber
Whereas to this game the Affable Lug
Lugged some serious lumber.

He started the game with a single,
Then stole bag number two.
No need now to ask yourself
What Johnny D would do.

Johnny held up as Manny's drive
Took a sec to safely pass Jeter.
Damon tore to the plate, the ball got their first
By a half a centimeter.

Damon's called out. Momentum shifts south,
At least that's what New York reckoned.
They basked in the glory of that shift
For about a nanosecond.

With Manny on, Ortiz makes Brown's first pitch
Do a noise like "Kablooie",
And sing as it clears the right field wall,
"Meet me in St. Loui!"

Top o' the second, two to zip
Papi's Homer still rattlin' the bleachers
Millar singles. Brown walks two guys
With hairy facial features;

Namely Mueller and Cabrera!
Brown was pitching hoary.
With two earned runs and three guys on
Brown gets Yanked by Torre.

Who brings in starter, Javier Vasquez
To strike out Johnny Damon,
Who might be giving serious thought
To where Javier'd be aimin'.

Johnny's thinking Vasquez is thinking
He's got to throw a fastball.
With three bags full of Red Sox
They can't afford a passed ball.

Vasquez is thinking Johnny's thinking
Posada's thinking curve,
Something with some trickiness,
Something to unnerve.

Posada's thinking Johnny's thinking
About not much at all,
For Johnny D proclaimed his team
"Idiots" one and all.

But Johnny's thinking that "idiot" thing
Was your classic reverse-double psych,
And a starting pitcher with bases full
Would attempt a fastball strike.

So Johnny creams that fastball
O'er bases fully manned!
Three Sox touch Home before he does!
That Slam is Mightily Grand!

'Tis a thing of Natural Beauty,
A thing of Awesome Pride
When Johnny gives that hurtin' ball
It's stratospheric ride!

Each Sox Fan Wills it out of there!
Pudge-Fisks that ball be Gone!
Fly over the Yankee Bullpen!
Fly over that outfield lawn!

Fly into Red Sox History!
Damon wills it most of all!
"Fly forever out of here
Before you start to fall."

In a championship context,
Grand Slams are really cool
'Cause they Rock the House that Ruth Built
From Attic to Vestibule.

Your uniforms stay nice and neat.
Obnoxious fans shut up!
<u>Plus</u> you get four nifty runs
And a Full-Team Dugout Hug-up!

Meanwhile Yankee bats are whiffin' air
Hairless faces looking crestfallen,
For Derek Lowe, in a post season groove
Is expertly sinkerballin'.

"Lowe and Behold" gets twenty-one outs,
Throwing just sixty-nine pitches
Forty-four of which are classic strikes
Thrown with guile that bewitches.

The Yankees sneak a run across
'Pon Jeter's third-inning single.
While the Sox earn themselves a Ballad,
Jeter gets nary a jingle.

In the top of the fourth, Cabrera walks,
Bringing up Johnny D,
Who'd shown that the more teammates on base,
The better his bat's repartee.

The Yanks are looking to maybe fine-tune
Vasquez's last pitch selection,
Recalling how far his last one had flown
In a right-field bleacher direction.

Damon clocks this one so mightily hard!
Resoundingly it gets Clouted.
It flies so far over the Yard
Everyone knew it was Outed!

When Damon the J-Man in This Seventh Game
Sees two pitches 'pon which he calls dibbies,
And Clocks them Afar with a Titan's Might,
It's Sweet! Two Swings! Six Ribbies!

When the Yanks get down eight to one
After four (count 'em four) short innings,
Their fans might well begin to doubt
Their aptitudinal underpinnings.

F'rinstance the guy in the right-field stands
Who yesterday yelled "Who's your daddy!?"
While hitting the dirt to duck Damon's Blast
Finds himself feeling less chatty!

Whereas the Sox are feelin' the Joy
Of Johnny Crankin' a Slam
And then a Twofer into the seat
For which that guy paid many a clam.

So many Sox are roundin' the bags
Francona gets a little dizzy.
He puts Pedro in to practice a little,
And the Yanks get a little busy.

Jeter singles to score two runs
A squibby thing curving askew,
Then Pedro gets through the seventh
Without any more whoop-de-do.

Boston-Born Bellhorn then Belts One Out
Accurate as Acupuncture!
(The Yanks are having Home Run Issues
At a Very Critical Juncture!)

Nixon hits neatly and then makes third.
The Sox not playing like Idjits.
Cabrera then drives a sacrifice fly,
Nixon's run scoring Double Digits.

Embree comes in to seal the win,
Pitching an awestriking dream,
Making the ball do goofy stuff
'Cause of how fingertips touch the seam.

The Final Yankee of Two-Thousand-Four
Bites Yankee Stadium dust!
In this Ten to Three Domination
Not a facial hair gets mussed.

The Jubilating Red Sox
Run Together to envelop
The Red Sox Celebration Thing
It took a Season to develop!

Celebrating crushing homers
And pitching wicked nifty.
What starts with just two high-fives
Becomes a High Two-Fifty.

They do the All-Team Hug-up
The Manny-Pedro Head-Mop Tussle
And that Cabrera-Ortiz Funky-Bop
That uses every single muscle.

And from that ballpark's excitation
This Jubilation Celebration
Spreads across All Red Sox Nation
A Joy of Endless Adoration.

The Baseball gods approve with nods
The Yankee onslaught thus withstood,
Bestow fair honor on the Sox
And deem and call it Good.

10. THE ONE-HUNDREDTH WORLD SERIES

The Hundredth World Series begins
October Twenty-Third,
The Sox's sox matching hues
With St. Louis's mascot bird.

The Cards had won one-hundred-five:
Most wins in all the Majors.
You'd think that Busch's turf would host Game One,
Not Boston's Golden-Ager's.

But thanks to Roger Clemens
Blown away in the All-Star Game
Giving up six to the Sox's League:
To Fenway Park they came.

Wakefield pitches a shut-out first:
So far the run total is bare
But when this game is over you have
More runs than facial hair.

'Cause Damon doubles. Cabrera gets hit.
Ortiz comes to bat with two on,
Smacks his hands, then smacks it out!
An October Phenomenon!

Millar then doubles. Mueller singles him in.
It's four to nothing, Sox.
In the third every guy on the Red Sox Team
Steps into the batter's box!

Mueller, Mirabelli, Bellhorn and Damon
Alternate walks and singles.
Cabrera and Manny then single as well!
Each run with fun commingles!

Two theories exist relevant to
Manny's outfield molestation,
(Details of which remain undisclosed
Pending investigation.)

(1) Manny was just adding levity
By taking an outfield seat;
Or (2) (From a very reliable source)
A sniper shot his cleat.

Whatever. He slides to catch the ball
And catches a cleat instead;
Adding to the effect of this are
His frolicking locks of dread.

The Sox keep hitting and get a bunch more,
But the Cardinals get a bunch too.
Tied nine to nine in the top of the eighth
What next will those playful gods do?

They'll bring Varitek up to bat
Who'd been solid behind that plate,
Who hits a grounder to Renteria
Just as solid at short stop. But wait!

The ball does a dipsy-doodly thing
Off Renteria's glove!
Jason tears safely to first on his error
For the Cards heretofore unheard of.

Bringing Bellhorn up to bat
Who'd homered in two games running,
Who belts a blast the wind carries foul
Not far from where he was gunning.

He fine-tunes with a blast the second pitch hence
Well over the head of Pujols.
That ball has fairness and plenty of airness
And smacks the Pesky Pole.

When you hit the Pesky Pole at the Fens;
When you hit it hard and fair;
The Fenway Fandom tends to go nuts
From their hats to their underwear!

They go nuts in Madawaska, Maine.
And around Narragansett Bay,
From Connecticut to Lake Champlain
They pull corks from fine Beaujolais!

As the Winning Pitch of Reliever Foulke
To the plate is swiftly unfurled,
Bellhorn's winning 11-9 Shot
Is heard around the World!

11. THE NINTH HEROIC TASK:
October 24th, 2004

A moist mist meets Mr. Taylor
As he sings the Anthem in Boston.
A Glistening Fenway seems dreamlike
On account of that Game Two frostin'.

Schilling's again throwing lightening
Throwing thunderbolts down from his Mount.
Beating gods of lesser Dieties;
Gods of lesser account.

Red, the Hue of the Noblest Heart,
Beats a badge into his sock.
Of Courage this Immortal knows,
This Heart in a Brain in a Jock.

Schilling's awesome, again, for six
Throwing fastballs, cutters and splitters.
The guy has written a separate book
On each of the Cardinal hitters.

The Sox hit two ground balls for outs.
Manny walks, Ortiz likewise.
Up to the deck steps Varitek
A pitch for to fragmentize.

Varitek waits on a change-up pitch,
And blasts it o'er Edmonds in center.
Two runs score! Jason slides into third!
The Fans couldn't be much contenter.

In the Fourth Mueller doubles with a mate on first,
Leaving Sox on second and third.
Then Bellhorn smacks one to center:
Two doubles by Sox less coiffured!

In the sixth, Cabrera powers a drive
Off a Big Green Wall out in left.
Two runs come in, as Schilling leaves
The Cardinals of runs near bereft.

Schilling had just a little help
From the Puckish gods of Fate;
Like you'd think the base path from first to third
One could easily navigate.

But Womack smacks one into the gap
With Sanders takin' off first
You'd figure if Sanders missed second base
It's the Cards that must be cursed.

But miss second base is what Sanders does.
Leaving Cards shy of second and third.
So when Matheny lines to Mueller
A rally is duly interred.

Schilling savors six sweet ones, then takes a rest,
The Sox winning six to one.
When Embree, Timlin and Foulke close the game
To the Cards 'tis a dart in the bun!

12. THE TENTH HEROIC TASK:
October 26th, 2004

Down 0 to two the Cards head to St. Lou
Where the home crowd treats 'em nicer.
Nary aware, what awaits them there
Is a Pedro Martinez Icer.

In the first Ramirez clobbers one out.
It's one to nothing, Sox.
St. Louis quickly gets feisty,
Right out of the batter's box.

Walker walks, as if that verb
Is somehow the root of his name.
Pujols rockets one off the glove of Mueller
Which single sets fans aflame.

Pedro walks Rolen. Three on in the first.
Edmonds knocks a short fly to Manny.
Walker tags and tears. Manny throws it home,
With accuracy that's uncanny.

Jason tags Walker for out number three,
Two feet shy of the Big Quesadilla!
Then in the third, Suppan singles,
Bringing up Renteria,

Who smacks a double off the right-field wall.
Pitcher Suppan stands on bag three.
Walker grounds to Bellhorn who tosses to first;
Out-wise, Walker's fricassee!

While over at third, Suppan has a choice.
He could tear home and score a run;
Or walk back to third and be safe thereat.
Most guys would choose number one.

But not Suppan, who picks option Three,
Which is: Fumble-Foot, Looking Hapless!
Stand twixt the bases, test the arm of Ortiz
'Till the base paths are rendered one chap less,

By a David Ortiz Laser Toss
That Smokes through the air straight to Mueller
Who slaps the tag! Suppan's wanderings cease!
The coach at third couldn't look iller.

A half-inning later, Sox up in the fourth;
Mueller hits the gap in left center.
He tears into second, gracefully.
The Sox again are contenter.

Trot Nixon singles! Mueller scores!
The Sox are up two to zip.
Strengthened by the Ortiz-Mueller Out,
Pedro asserts stewardship!

Martinez takes off on this Gift from the gods
Seven innings! Three hits, seven K!
Fifty-nine strikes, twenty-one outs!
Pitch-wise, this guy is Fillet.

Then in the fifth Damon Doubles!
Cabrera singles him to third!
Manny singles a Johnny-D-Batted-In
Varitek hits a non-sequitured.

By which is meant, Jason beats the throw
Of the force-out ball that gets Manny.
Then Mueller singles one that would have scored
Orlando Cabrera's Granny!

With two runs in the fifth, it's four to zip.
Pedro leaves after seven a hero.
For every Cardinal frame at bat
The scoreboard records a zero.

Timlin throws hard; three up—three down;
A perfect Inning Eight;
Then Foulke strikes out Renteria,
To keep perfect his E.R. Rate.

But a solo home-run by Walker
Soils Foulke's E.R.A. by a dite.
Pujols then flies to deep left for an out;
Foulke strikes out Rolen! Good Night!

13. THE ELEVENTH AND FINAL HEROIC TASK: *October 27, 2004*

<u>Good</u> News for St. Lou: There is one team
That's come back from three games to donut.
The <u>Bad</u> News is, that that one team
Is their Red-Socked, current opponut!

A mere four pitches into Game Four
Damon swings at the two and one;
Cranking pitch four for a homer to right!
Fourth pitch; Game-Winning Run!

Womack then singles off of Lowe
To start the Cardinal first.
Walker's bunt then moves him on;
To second he quickly traversed.

Then Pujols grounds him o'er to third
On Bellhorn's toss to Ortiz.
But Rolen's nubber is grabbed by Lowe,
Who tags out Rolen with ease.

The Red Sox third is a whole team thing,
Lowe's sinker dartin' like a weasel,
Knowin' the Cards can't get the runs
That the Red Sox and Ortiz'll!

A one-out single by Manny
Precedes an Ortiz double.
Pujols throws home a Varitek smash
Manny's out by some facial stubble.

Two outs to Mueller who draws a walk
To join Jason and David on base.
Trot Nixon swings on a three and O
And misses a Slam by an Ace.

The little green monster in Center at Busch
Gets slammed, and gets slammed hard!
Two runs trot home on Trot's two-bagger
Just a tad from out of the Yard!

Time for the "Hold" part of "Lowe and Behold."
And at the risk of sounding boring,
That double by Nixon concluded
One-Hundredth World Series Scoring.

Lowe's Pitcher Perfect, so's the Pen.
The Cards are matched against Heroes.
Through nine full innings, Cards have nothing to show
'Exceptin' nine empty zeros.

The ninth goes up when Foulke underflips
The Baseball to Mientkiewicz!
BoSox Fans go Bonkers All Over
Nationwide Bailiwicks!

While in the in-field at St. Lou,
Such a Beautiful Celebration
Is shown around to All the World
By Telecommunication.

Manny in left eyes a line to this Joy
Like a runway to Arroyo's Hair Corn.
At a sprint to this Love-In he picks up speed
And at three feet out gets Airborne!

He flies for Joy above this Bunch
Who's Heart and Athleticism
Brought them to this Lofty Place
Of Victory's Sweet Aestheticism!

The Beauty of this Squeezin' Scrum
Is placed at No Small Risk
When Dave Ortiz Goes Airborne!
The Sox Doc thinks: Spinal Disc

Of whomever is where Ortiz comes down!
Here's hoping he's got a good back!
And takes just a moment to brace and grab
His sacroiliac!

The earthiness of such worldly thought
Is belied by their Jubilant Flight!
They'd come from afar, battled and won
To Reach this Hallowed Height!

As sure as the maples turn gold in the fall,
And the snow falls shortly thereafter,
Endorphins you feel at the sight of this scrum
Are the same as from love or laughter.

For who conceived, other than These
Such a Clear Heroic Story
That will Stand the Test of Ages to Come
In the Light of This Team's Glory?

'Twas a Miracle brought together
These Men of Majestic Might
Who fit the Means to Boston's Dreams
Of Victory's Radiant Light.

Olympus smiles upon these Men,
And wishes to bear them up
To this Mount of the gods, and offer them Drink
From Immortality's Cup.

For they've Earned the Things Most Beautiful.
Fought for Something Divine!
Resurrected, from fully three games down
A Life of Grand Design!

For Heroes are they who Battle this Beast
That's plundered their Homeland for years,
And with Nobleness, bring Home its Heart
As proof for the Balladeers!

14. RETURN TO THE HOMELAND'S JUBILANT PARADE

To Home: the Base of the Jewel at the Fens
Where on April sixteenth, 'aught four
The Sox whupped the Yankees six runs to two
To Start this Journey of Lore.

To Home this Song of Adventure
That their Souls in Spring decreed
Would overcome perils and obstacles
By Noble Heart and Deed.

The Majestic Parade of Autumn earned
By men trusted to carry this Spirit.
Greatness brought Home, bestowing Life
'Pon Fans who'll forever revere it!

Sweet Dreams, my Children,
For now you've heard
Of a Team and a Towne
And of Guys rounding third!

Of the Guys on This Team
Rounding third the Most
All Season Long,
And right through the Post.

Of Wicked Good Pitching
Of a Faithful Unwavered
Even when Yankees
Up three-zip were favored.

Of Greatness Achieved
By One Team full of Men
Who'd like real soon
To do it again.

And a Towne full of History
Sports-wise and More
Born Again and Forever
In Two Thousand Four.

THE END

About the Ballad

The 2004 World Championship was the most magical story in the history of Boston Baseball. Set largely in historic Fenway Park, this Ballad paints the picture of true glory and team greatness, combining exciting and memorable play-by-play action with a mythological perspective.

Readers will delight in the author's nimble wit and wordplay, that bring history, poetry, sports entertainment and humor to these pages.

About the Author

Dan Bates is a Red Sox Fan with a Muse and a Thesaurus. His Muse: Beth, his Beloved. His Thesaurus: Roget's. The Ballad of the Beantowne Bosox is the third sports ballad by the author; the first being the Ballad of Danny the Deckape (re: sailboat racing), delivered to the crew of the Apogee at the All-Dave Dinner in Harpswell; and the second the Ballad of Whizzer the Warthog (re: Cumberland, Maine Recreational Soccer) delivered at the Warthogs' Award Pizza Banquet in the Cumberland Congregational Church Gym. Both unpublished, but funny'r'n' a Yank wailing at a Wakefield Knuckler!

978-0-595-39456-2
0-595-39456-6

Printed in the United States
59681LVS00006B/169